Folding

Folding a River

Tawona Sitholé and Alison Phipps

wild goose
publications

www.**iona**books.com

First published 2026 by
Wild Goose Publications
Suite 9, Fairfield
1048 Govan Road, Glasgow G51 4XS, Scotland
A division of Iona Community Trading CIC
Limited Company Reg. No. SC156678
www.ionabooks.com

ISBN 978-1-80432-393-9

Cover photo and interior photos © Tawona Sitholé

Printed in the UK by Page Bros (Norwich) Ltd

◆ Contents ◆

Part III – Freedom to wonder

Part IV – Freedom to bear

Part V – Freedom to praise

Epilogue – Warriors cry

This collection is dedicated to the spirit,
wisdom and courage of migrating peoples

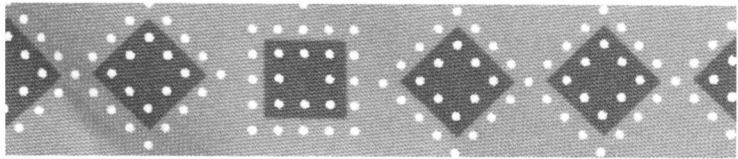

Introduction

This anthology is a sequel to *The Warriors Who Do Not Fight* (2018), our first joint collection. In that collection we were keen as poets and colleagues working on common tasks in intercultural research and the arts to respond to the crises in global migration. The promptings into poetry came from different, yet complementary, traditions and experiences. The poetry in this anthology moves deeper into the conflicts and concerns surfacing in our work since the publication of *The Warriors Who Do Not Fight*.

The poetry comes from the experience of many lands and many journeys. These journeys, whilst suffused with beauty, are also encounters with the tangible suffering caused by inequality, misdirections in development, and deliberate forms of violence. The violence of poverty, gender-based violence, migratory violence, border violence and the violations of culture, language, nature, bodies; the violences of war.

It is important for us to be able to act as poet- and scholar-celebrants in gatherings of distress and questioning, curiosity and despair. This anthology offers a window into our daily work. It shows how we see our own often ceremonial, dramaturgical or liturgical anchoring practice in teaching, research and peacebuilding, where the poems take on life.

The anthology is structured into five parts, each inspired by a freedom aspired to in the Universal Declaration of Human Rights and in the Sustainable Development Goals. These are freedoms, documented in many international instruments, which shape the work undertaken by the UNESCO Chair for Refugee Integration through Education, Languages and the Arts at the University of Glasgow. This is work for peace and for integral human development, for the dignity of the human person, for restorative integration and a just, sustaining peace.

These international instruments have framed the design of our research and project work in Ghana, Palestine and the Gaza Strip, Morocco, Zimbabwe, Mexico, Scotland, Haiti, Brazil, Jordan, Egypt, Malaysia, Nepal, Ethiopia, South Africa, China, Burkina Faso, Côte d'Ivoire, Eritrea, Aotearoa New Zealand, Australia and Canada.

The instruments, however, are very much part of human solutions to human-made problems and our work sets these in a wider context of accountability to the more-than-human-world, to the earth and creative forces that nourish and sustain. In short, the work that this anthology has come from aims to 'hold the bowl of tears and expand the space for joy' (Kahlil Gibran). In this respect we see the poems and anthology itself as vessels, or containers – calabash, quaich, hari, deze we call them in the varied languages of our work.

Our poetry has been formed through encounter as ceremony, dramaturgy and liturgy, containing the traces of pain and possibility that are at the root of yearnings for courage and freedom.

These poems stem from our work from 2017-2024.

* We have differentiated authorship by font. The first poem in the collection is by Alison, the responding poem by Tawona, and so on.

A note on the cover image and illustrations

The cover and illustrations in this book are photographs of a *retso*, the name given to the patterns in the cloth worn by hunters and warriors, nomads and gatherers in southern African traditions.

A *retso* represents the spirit of endeavour and wrestling with problems, coming literally to terms with them in our own endeavour. It represents the spirit of nomadic hunters, adventurers, providers, respectful of the lands they cross and the spirit of the lands and their custodians, whilst practising risk-taking and discovering how to live with both scarcity and abundance.

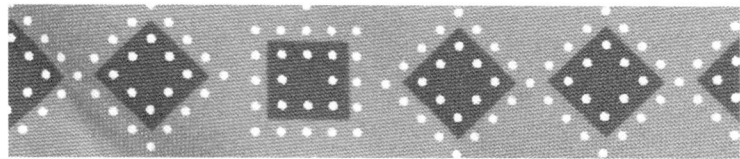

Part I – Freedom to move

Labyrinth

Just begin.

Place one foot in front of the other.

Walk.

Walk slowly.

Or run if you would feel the wind
play tricks from all directions.

Just begin.
Walk.
Watch your feet.

Or the trees.
Or the sky.
Or the bright dots
that are flowers.

Just begin.

The path chooses you.
Follow her calling.
Watch as she curves
and moves
and shows new vistas.

Just begin and walk.
At dawn.
At dusk.
In the midday sun.
Or under the stars.

Notice.
Just notice,
the way the path turns,
and you turn,
and the world turns.

Commissioned for the Dyce Park Labyrinth, Partick, Glasgow

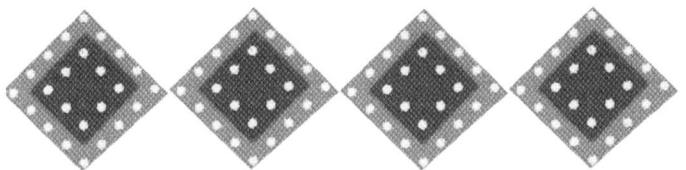

a guide to the traveller

the traveller is a fascinating creature
noticeable by distinct marks and markings
noticeable by distinct noises and sounds
behaviours and oddities
traits and qualities
adaptable to different conditions
and habitats
able not only to survive but thrive
the traveller is a remarkable creature

depending on conditions
the traveller will
amble or rumble
scramble or gamble
gallop or gather
climb or claw
depending on conditions
the traveller will
fly or defy
spoil or recoil
leap or sleep
lead or stampede
depending on conditions
the traveller
follows or is followed

depending on conditions
it's a matter of

hiding or deciding
wading or waiting
depending on conditions
it's a matter of
a clear path
or
clear the path

along the life long journey
there are many places
the traveller will reach
before arriving

muganhu
depending on conditions
can be common
middle
or battle
ground
zambuko
depending on conditions
can be a breeze
squeeze
or
freeze

there is time for the sublime
but it also brings a curse
there is time for the sunshine
but it also brings thirst

depending on conditions
the traveller is
prepared or scared
alone or among
gurusvusvu
ngongoni
mbizi
nekacheche
gurusvusvu

depending on no conditions
in the making of the journey
mapping of the journey
marking of the journey
the heart leaves distinct footprints

Commissioned by Glasgow Life for the Commonwealth Games, 2014

Obedience

I spent the day in obedience.
Unwriting all that has been written.
Unwalking the beech-strewn paths.
Unthinking all that has been thought.
Unfeeling all sensuous sensation.
I let the water lap around my skin
then unlapping, let the water join the mist.
I held only air.
Spoke only with silence.
Touched only where the shadows lay.
I reeled in every prayer,
unhooked the bait,
threw the fish back into the water.
Decreated, I surveyed the battlefield.
Warriors are not warriors outwith wartime.
Warriors are gardeners,
poets,
spirits of the living,
spirits at one
with the dead.
Decreated, I tore the many words from my lips,
the many thoughts from my mind,
the many hopes from my heart.
Decreated, I left the dance floor.
And for a while
my land had rest from war.

First published in Decolonising Multilingualism: Struggles to Decreate,
Multilingual Matters, Bristol, 2019

leopard hunter

in untamed forests
of unheard sounds
roam unknown displays
of unnerving prey
in unkempt spaces
on unearthed ground
flicker unlit firesides
of unheld gatherings
in unseen worlds
of unspoken words
the unfurling taile
of the leopard hunter

*tail/tale: This is lost in performance and rendered here as taile to hold the
oral integrity and offer clarity to readers.*

What is your peace?

In commissions for the future
you have found your peace awaken
made of pieces from a past
and strong objects that were taken

objects taken from the firesides
objects stolen from the land
that were hidden in a language
and then given a tourist brand.

Are you angry in the darkness
are you carving the words that tell
have you found a place for tragedy
where lonely warriors fell?

For now they have a Kitemark
and a date stamp
and an author
an auctioneer
a profiteer,
a collector
and curator.

Is your peace stored in an archive
with a long translated glossary
typewritten in an English
with a 'scholars only' policy?

Have you found it
in the cabinets

on shelving
in the dust?

Is it bubble-wrapped
or padlocked
or simply left to rust?

Is it hopeless
is it restless
is it marked
as highly dangerous?

Is it curious,
furious,
or with a label
that is spurious?

Are you learning of its meaning
have you touched the life it lost?
Are you testing it for dreaming
have you read of what it cost?

Is your piece held in a ribcage
that can hear the war songs singing
of the ones who cross the ages
and seek out your tongue's own drumming?

Are you angry in the darkness
are you carving the words that tell
have you found a place for tragedy
where lonely warriors fell?

our squinty house

what is the foundation
of this house
this building
is it a ruwaré
a hard place suitable for beginners
or is it mumvura
a fluid space perfect for wanderers
depends on the conditions
depends on the builders
what are the materials
for this building
respect skill passion risk
compassion creativity
humility
listening listening listening listening
depends on the conditions
depends on the builders
having so many builders
there are no right angles
having so many windows
there are no wrong angles
in this squinty house
it is just different angles
what is the making
of this house
making time
making a difference
making room
depends on the conditions

depends on the builders
in this building
sometimes you stand
sometimes you have to stoop
sometimes you speak
sometimes you have to whoop
sometimes in frustration
you feel like calling the builder
but it's your own name that rings
sometimes you sit alone
sometimes cram together
home is where we rest
home is where we wrestle
this building be a tree
that bends with the wind
in the many many storms
the spirit must be
aya the resilient
in this house
who are the builders
what are the conditions

Written for the MIDEQ symposium, 5 February, 2021, South-South Migration Inequality and Development Hub. The poem explores a metaphor for the project of development proposed by Professor Heaven Crawley.

With holding

With holding
or
Withholding
war.

second handling

if
carefully
maintained
usually
one
cannot
easily
distinguish
between
used
and
knew

We are freer than we believe

'We are freer than we believe'
he said,
incarnating the world as refuge,
requiring the enfleshment of spirit,
respiriting the earth,
offering love to the water,
     the river,
         the sea.

b is for black, c is for captain: alphabet-themed misadventures of a terribly seasick crew with stoic colonial disposition in unrelenting tidal waves of historical inadequacies

these seas swirl fires
and beasts to tame
dark lands with dangers and
treasures unknown
to err may recur but swear
to recall
good lords and ladies
and thrones to obey

aye aye captain

if only you could see your ship now
storms have been plenty
still i've honoured your orders
cool as watermelon
learnt to read and write
but cannot 'rithmetic my way
out of the hold of your ship

Written for the exhibition 'Call and Responses: The University of Glasgow and Slavery', for Dr Christine Whyte, Beniba Centre, University of Glasgow. The 26-word title is a mischievous nod to the word limit in the commission brief.

The waiting

All those agonising years,
the centuries of living with a punitive father
and no mother at all,
of endlessly hearing the same
unpopular priests and prophets
telling it straight
to a wanton people,
and their being right,
always,
in the end.

All the false starts with men's systems
of monarchies and judges,
all the walls built only to fall again,
all the fiery furnaces
and lions,
the whales and animal arks,
which were sent as stories
to hearts of stone.

When all it took was a woman's story
of a heart of flesh,
consenting to the question,
in a world where previously
there was no right to the question,
when all it took was a woman's story
of a stranger making room,

when room was scarce
and fear was high
and every moving living thing
was to be counted
and taxed
for breathing, for dwelling.

When all it took was a woman's story
of birth,
of the first cry,
with the first breath,
and the first home,
in the first arms
of the woman,
who was the mother,
and the father,
who was not.
That's all.
That's the story.
That's all it takes
for milk to flow,
and honey.

Therefore, let us keep the feast.

rukweza farmer

vakuru vakati
pasi kare makunguo aidyei
here
bestowed the honour
i now have a choice
of spending, taking or playing with time
precisely 1 hour 15 minutes
i turn to the timely tone of timelessness
return to the wilderness of imagination
the rukweza farmer sits
guarding the precious rukweza crop
guarding against makunguo
the winged intruders who disrupt
to steal the precious rukweza crop
and yet shumo the proverb
finds us in question
pasi kare makunguo aidyei
in the absence of the farmer's field
what do makunguo eat
vakuru vakati
kurodza demo hakutambisi nguva
the rukweza farmer sits still
the rukweza farmer sits in silence
and yet shumo the proverb
is not out of the question
kurodza demo hakutambisi nguva
silence is not wasting time
it is preparation for speaking
stillness is not wasting time
it is preparation for action

the rukweza sways in the wind
but is confined
to the farmer's field
the rukweza is kissed by the sun
but it was not the caress of the wind
that brought it here
here
the rukweza does not grow wild
here
language does not grow wild
it is restrained by tenses
confined
to the farmer's field
the manicured field of grammar
and yet shumo the proverb
remains in question
pasichigaré
ancestors are not in the past present or future
ancestors are boundless
in the wilderness of imagination
in storytelling
in mbira melodies
rukweza is not tamed into a crop
rukweza grows wild here
here in
pasichigaré

Part II – Freedom to create

Warrior bird

The robin is the warrior of the birds.
Breast painted vermilion.
Cloaked in branches.
Strong in visage.
Bright black daystar of an eye.
Daring me with his closeness
to my earth, my rake, my garden.
Taking the food
from the turn of my spade.
Holding his tune by my ear.
Reminding me that the
earth is mine

not at all.

forest songs

as travellers strive
from origin to destiny
there's a little bird
who wings the forest

in familiar landscape
or don't know the way
there's a little bird
who pings the forest

tired and hungry
worried and thirsty
there's a little bird
who brings the forest

as different truths
fight over her name
there's a little bird
who kings the forest

a medium connecting
worlds to other worlds
there's a little bird
who swings the forest

from ancient times
travellers have known
there's a little bird
who sings the forest

Silence

Conversation is what
we are made for,
that there may be words between
us, honest speech, the framing of pain
in between tongue and teeth.
The greeting of day, of night.
The telling of news, of joy.

The silence offers punctuation.
[…]
Days of punctuation.

Here, though, a chance to wait
(in the brackets), listening intently
to what will become of the absent
words.

Is this the silence of war?

Will the next words announce a truce
or a resumption of the wounding,
or the chance of embrace of
loved ones, behind the doors
and in safety,
where warriors cry,
cleaning the wounds with
greetings of tears,

where speech may be,
what speech needs to be:

Protest.
Punctuation.
Praise.

speaky clean

there are countless nuggets
in mind and unmined
made of the wisdom of silence
words being overrated
roots being underrated
how treacherous this
spoken path
how strenuous this
chosen path
that chooses me

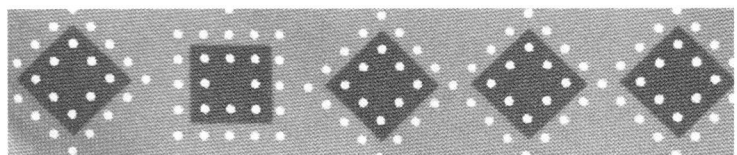

Wanted

It is every sign of wanting
that finds me wanting.

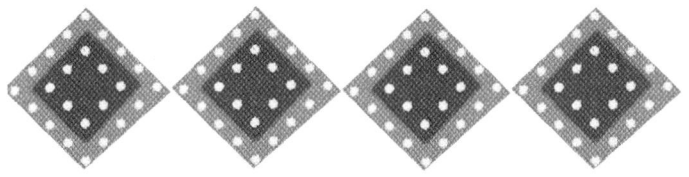

handmade

weavers weave us
weavers leave us
what we need to carry
what we need to carry

There is also this to tell

There is also this to tell:
I miss the greetings,
the certainty of presence
beginning and ending the day.

I miss the laughter,
the care,
the gentle company,
the way I could reach for your wisdom.

I miss the smiles.

The necessity for protection and priority
gives reason all power.

To know the power of reason is
to know and find respect
for the wild things.
It is diminishment and discipline.
It is necessary cost.
We understand
standing under
its authoritative voice.

Nature retreats to a safe distance.

In the language of poetry
there is also this to tell –

the power and victory of reason
is not where our arrows were made,
is not the fire where they wait
for the warrior's skin.

Reason is not our war story.

maybe it is

there is no one else here but i'm not alone
i don't understand what i know
but maybe it is wisdom
i shiver a little
i shudder a little
in the grip of mysterious claws
the sweep of mysterious feathers
taking me by surprise to the forest of my thoughts
made of flames and rain and wind and dark and bones and
light
and to the battlefield
and the resting place
the cause of my wounds
and the well of healing
perhaps it is *super*vision
to see hate and still keep love
to feel power and still stay humble
to prize valuables and still hold values
i don't understand what i know
but maybe it is wisdom
i don't understand what i see
but maybe it is *super*vision
the grip of claws
sweep of feathers
i shiver a little
i shudder a little

ndaifunga kuti ndapedzeredza
ndichiti aiwa ndacherechedza
kwanzi maisokwadzo
nyemba kutsva dzarungwa
ivo vekanye vakareketa
chiri mumoyo chiri mudima
ndini ganyamatope dzapasi changamire
gwenyambira musango
idzo pwere
icho charinga
ndaifunga kuti ndapedzeredza
asi nganga yaakuringa pasi

shiri yakanaka unoendepi

Commissioned for 'Angels' Exhibition, Glasgow Life, September 2015

The one I am

I am in the air,
the tree,
the bare feet
and the stone.
I am in the muchakata fruit,
the pages of the book,
the soft speech and song.

I am here to calm storms
and storm the calm.

I am twist and turbulence.
I am music and movement.
I bring harmony and healing
and a war of feeling
to your breast.

Your breast.

I am red and GreenBlue.
I am skinned and boned.
I am riddle and rhythm.
I am not afraid
but longing
to understand.

I am praise and possibility.
I am none of these things.

I am the dancer in the flame
and the flame of the dance.
I am the taker of your breath
and the giver of your breathing.

So tell me, my soul's mater
and meet-er;
tell me, wearer of wounds and scars;
tell me, holder of hand blessings
and care-taker;
tell me, maker of ways and encounters;
weaver of enchantment and entrancements;
tell me, what are you singing,
what is the music of this meeting?

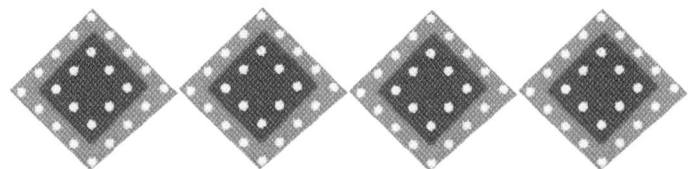

sleeping awake

changana ngechangana
chesango mutoro wamambo

last night i slept awake
i slept awake last night
at first it was the noise
coming from the corridor
and when that died down
an odour began to take over
a silent irritation
emanating from unpicked fruit
rotting on the vine
and even when that cleared
i still could not drift off
bereft of lightness
left navigating by fading signs
through human traffic
splishsplashsploshing
in the driving rain
and even when that waned
bereft of brightness
left recollecting memorabilia
hidden in the hapHazard
of overcrowded questions
keep scuffling scuffling
keep shuffling shuffling
my deck of playing cards
my own make-believe tarot

a chance mystic reading
of language and information
fuelling this gruelling duelling
combatants as ever *en garde*
sworn in the protectorate
combatants as ever on guard
sworn to the electorate
sold to the scratchcard hype
of humans becoming smarter over time
and over time
fixated dreams remain broken
dictated notes remain token
infected wounds remain open
and i remain annoyingly woken
perhaps pure excitement
perhaps mere consequence
of exposure
perhaps i'm dressed too thin
for the northern tropic
perhaps i'm dressed too thick
for the southern tropic
whatever the disturbing topic
last night i slept awake
unable to keep my eyes open
unwilling to keep my eyes shut

changana ngechangana
chesango mutoro wamambo

Written for Seng Guan and the Malaysia team at the MIDEQ project

I remember writing my first poem

For Alison

I remember writing
my first poem
all trembly
because words
had found me out.

And these words
find you out
and open you up
and offer you strength
and serve up your vulnerability

and the form reveals your
soft underbelly
your strong shell.

The longer lines,
the sudden rhymes,
the lingering, loveliness of words,
words which are strangers
words which are friends.

emissions

every day we wake we make
history
every way we relate we create
emissions
toxins and pollutants
that contaminate the atmosphere
and it all builds up
rising tempers
storms of emotions
floods of tears
we will need to feel safe
family or friend
neighbour or teacher
we all need to feel safe
the choice is ours
the power is ours
it's all about emissions
we create every day
these little emissions
we call words

For Dr Maureen Farrell, stalwart of National Poetry Day, School of Education, University of Glasgow, October 5th, 2023

Part III – Freedom to wonder

WindCalm

WindCalm,
under the
WidestBlueSkies
I ever have seen.
QuietSlowedFoot
at GeeseRising
at GooseFall.
DwellingPlaceofKnowledges
at GooseCall.
Recalled
Found
QuieteningSlowingFoot
BluingWideningSkies
WindCalming
GeeseCalling
GeeseCalming
WindCalling
FourDirections.

The NounsMakingForm of this poem, and some other poems, is in direct homage to the innovations in the abundance of possibilities of languages of our esteemed colleague Professor Kofi Anyidoho, Africa's leading scholar of poetry and the humanities.

*think*walking

thinking is a kind of walking
staying in step with passers-by
or coursing against the
concurring current of calm waters
and it's a long way down
from this lonely height where
this rickety footing is just an
expensive way of being honest
loud is the mouth of this river
as it snakes and shakes
itself into cupped hands
chapped hands choking with
untaken footsteps and the
tiring tirades of a tidal sea
and who should swirl here but a
whirlpool wonder woman
whose legend is passed
has been passed round
to me by me through me
a trusty tale to believe in
that *think*walking is not just a
raging river running slow
but bangled wrist ever watchful
timeful like the fireside circle
where inner strength is forged as
story of memory and the 'what if'
that decides the strides of you and i
now and ever then as it were
that taboo of us is just a
shocking walking superstition

For the Loud Poets, Edinburgh

When

I go to the mountains.
It is all energy.
When it's ready.
When you are ready.
You will be healed.

there are things

there are questions
and concerns
there is thinking
and in turn
there is action
and reflection
there is searching
in researching
and also
there are things
things that appear clear
and things that are opaque
things we will miss
and things we will mistake
there are these
there are things

At GorseBloom

Consider the silence
at GorseBloom.

An evergreen promise
of a thousand yellow kisses
interrupting even
the lark's clear air.

Each petal
a pause
taking
breath
away
until the tongue
makes her way
into praise.

Perhaps every word requires
the IceCrack
of the river at SpringMelt

the ShyBlush
of BloodRush at HeartMelt

the SkinShiver when
eyes
linger
long

with questions.

The silence
of GorseBloom,

mistress
of punctuation.

rootikali korekt

a petal that ignores the root
may radiate much dazzle
but will never really blossom
left out of bloom
precariously pretty
in a lowly height
lonely height
unfamiliar ground
oh to be grounded
how down
how deep
how far
far cry from a distant land
calling names
of branches and stalks
leaves and stems
flowers and shoots
fruits
and one more in providence
for the ones just budding
get together as a family
tree parts all held up
hearts all held together
by the roots

Abyss

In my tradition
there is a story of a refiner,
holding gold in the flame
until it reaches
its ultimate point of purification,
and then

knowing

when.

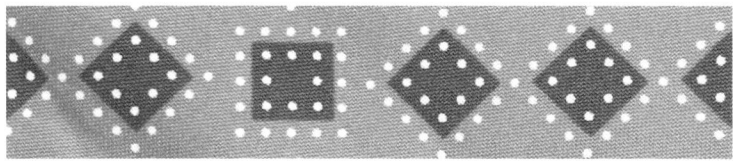

four fires

trembling

not with fear
but within
from fire
unfelt
unless
until

eruption

not in rage
but intensity
of fire
rising
setting
uprising

upsetting

not of mood
but offering
of fire
garnering
gathering
at dusty feat

of storytellers

At my lips

A great cup of healing.
At my lips
in my throat
reaching the blood in my heart
the marrow in my bones.

Then they added the poison
and let it linger through the veins.

Then they took the cup away.

And she withered.
Whole beeches died.
Rotted, fell into the
cold damp earth.

No fruit could come
from this root stock now.

No graft could take hold.

In spring a flower appeared,
hopeful.

But the cup had been broken
into a thousand tiny shards.

And they used each one to
cut down the flower,

scrape off the skin,
feed on the marrow,
dig a grave for her every bone.

It is wartime.

i don't need anything

i don't need a racist
no
i already have a tribalist
someone dedicated
to shaming our humanity

i don't need an enemy
please
i already have a friend
who else but who else can
unleash friendly fire

i don't need small-minded
at all
i already have big-headed
ready to gun me run me down
in a bullet train of thought

i don't need a problem
uh-uh
i already have a solution

corridors to other corridors
corridors with no doors

i don't need any extra
whatsoever
i already have enough
bullish at the buffet
and helpings aren't helping

i don't need you
sorry
i already have me
just a content individual
being selfish to the self

i don't need any of these
haikona
no thanks no rest
needs keep needing
wants keep wanting

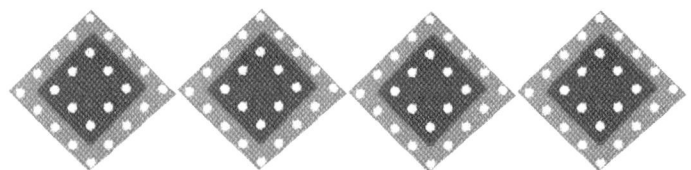

I want to make more time for roses

I want to make more time for roses;
that they will ramble over my frame
and feed on my love of them;
that in their budding
they will shyly brush my cheek;
and in full florid flower
they will smother me with their scent;
that when the storm comes and they bow their heads
damp and mouldering earthwards
that they will mingle raindrops with my tears;
and there will be salt on their petals
and rosewater on my skin.

Until gravity
pulls their touch onto
my arching, aching body,
as one with this good green groaning growing earth.

At PetalFall.

As petals fall.

As flowers turn
to rose hips.
Rising hips

GreenRed,

reddening into sweetness.

Entering
as rose wine.

how beautiful is life

For Donald and Maureen

family and friends
if only i was a yogi
i could take any form
the meditative
lotus
the energising
half lord of the fishes
or the common
downward facing dog
on this occasion
i will mostly remain in the
intoxicating
bent elbow pose
reflecting
how beautiful is life
when all is in perfect balance
strength grace and poise
and before my swagger
turns into a stagger
i want to invite you all
to chant hekani
hekani
and celebrate this moment
this gathering
reflecting
how beautiful is life

when we depend on structures
and rely on logic
yet the heart of the matter
is a matter of heart
but what can i tell anyone
about this thing called love
that brought us here
reflecting
how beautiful is life
how precious
when it has been to the brink
and back
how beautiful is life
when it is a shared struggle
a shared resilience
a shared celebration
never mind the contradictions
one person's barbecue
is another one's braai
and talking about rain
in Zimbabwe we long for it
and in Scotland
in Scotland
don't talk about rain
but please allow me
just for a moment
to talk about rain
reflecting
how beautiful is life
when the rains fall

and yet sometimes
the rains fail
sometimes
i see a vivid image
of a long line of women
in a familiar yoga pose
returning from the source
in perfect balance
strength grace and poise
reflecting
how beautiful is life
when the rains fall
and yet sometimes
the rains fail
sometimes
you just want to call out
amai hwè
sometimes
you just want to call out
chigutiro
tamba wakaguta
chigutiro
tamba wakaguta
hukamai
hunenge husahwira
hukamai

hunenge husahwira

Part IV – Freedom to bear

In that garden

And carefully,
in that garden,
with its walls of fruit trees
facing south,
and its scented herbs
for flavouring the healing,
the apple trees will witness the stories
and offer petals
to dress the uncovered wounds.
And the air will delight
in the mingling of hell with Heaven.
And pain will know why
she was born on the skin.

Born muting the now
unfettered tongue.

meticulous the gardener

that plant is a weed

meticulous the gardener
decides with no hesitation
growing where it shouldn't
so of kukosha
having none
so here come
necessary tools for necessary
hacking
hacking
digging
digging
that plant
of a thriving population
born of wind pollination
grounded such thing
earthed by totem being
a weed for weeding
and to do it properly
have to pull from the roots
and that's the land cleared

this plant is a plant

meticulous the gardener
knows with no investigation
growing there it should
and of kukosha
having tonnes

so here come
necessary tools for necessary
tending
tending
fencing
fencing
this plant
of promising signs
born of meticulous design
founded such thing
birthed by human being
a plant for planting
and to do it properly
have to pool from the youth
and that's the land developed

this plant that is rooted not in soil
this plant that stems not from seed
this plant that branches not for light
this seedling that is not a sibling
of scattered fellow earthlings

although raw materials will be ripening as it grows
so is this then what develop meant

this plant that does not dance in the wind
this plant that does not drink in the rain
this plant that does not eat in the sun
this plant that does not
catch brushstrokes of the seasons

although raw materials will be ripening as it grows
so is this then what develop meant

this plant that is not
a free and open source
no nourish flourish lively lush
just fizzy dizzy busy buzz
of worker drones
striving in dependence of this growth
expansionextensionextensionexpansion
expansionextensionextensionexpansion
playing on repeat
like songs
mighty mighty songs
of revolution
with a dreamy melody
sung from lips not from heart

by growth wishers shedding skin
for eeky strangers within
haplessly knocking shins
in a graceless jig

going
villainvictimvillainvictim
villainvictimvillainvictim
in this graceless jig

the day is done

meticulous the gardener
declares with no reservation
after an industrious time
*a*counting ripe materials
and of kukosha
who can say

earth is earth
nature is nature
a plant is a plant
a human being
hmmm
is something else

Written for 'Enough', a project of the Centre for Human Ecology

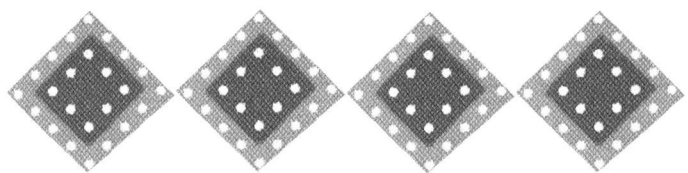

It's time

'It's time,' said the earth.
'It's time.
Come close.
Now lower yourself down
and into my embrace.
See, the light has returned.
Rub your hands, your cheek
against my smooth crumbling skin.
My scent is rising.
The sap is high.
Touch me.
Let your mind wander towards my fruits.
The hands full of red berries you will pluck
from these tiny green shoots.
The smooth-skinned wonders
that will push through the earth.
Be mine, be the earth you are.
Leave behind the earth longing of winter.
The feverish delirious desire for the soul.
The hours spent gazing after me
at the fireside and in the wool wind.
The snow has melted.
I am ready.
You and I, in this spring season,
we belong entwined,
entangled.'

show and tell

an unforgettable sunshine ago
pasi denga and mhepo came together
one said and one echoed the other
one said and one echoed the other
and after a while it was settled
regarding the gathering
being grounded
pasi was the natural
to host
being open
denga was the natural
to witness
being clear
mhepo was the natural
to take the message
to all the elders
so began preparation
one did and one echoed the other
one did and one echoed the other
and after a while it was settled
regarding the gathering
and so came the day
the elders were happy
regarding the gathering
Oak
Rowan
Pine
were happy

Baobab
Odum
Nahla
were happy
Guayacán
Matai
Mutohwe
were happy
and many many more
were happy

regarding the gathering
all who were to be fed
were nourished
all who were to be made
were crafted
all who were to be sheltered
were shaded
all who were to be healed
were treated
and so it remains
one says and one echoes the other
one does and one echoes the other
and so it remains settled
regarding the gathering

Star Earth

It was as if the night sky
had given his stars
to the meadows of spring.

Wings lap and a river is born in the sky
calling calling calling.
Each bubble,
each wave
each ripple and rapid
a flying brown fish
breathing the air.

Strewn across the
first fresh leaves of
lady's mantle
the bloodied birth sack
of a suckling lamb.

Under the copse of birch
and larch barely daring
to put on the green,
BlackVelvetHorned
roe deer
search out the bark.

a breath of myst

as stars on a black backdrop
the banner boldly twinkles

'i want to fill this town with artists'

i am taking in
i am taken in
a breath of myst
thrust through thresholds
as aura
as ritual
as wonderment
learning by spirit
guides in the guise of children
learning not to overestimate
the power of words
learning not to underestimate
the power of words
i find myself again
in a breath of myst
as shape-finding in clouds
eyes cannot see themselves
until faced with reflection
as music of forest sounds
ears cannot hear themselves
until placed in immersion
as aura
as ritual

as wonderment
later that evening
as i crossed another bridge
the colour of the river
was a swallowing silver

Folding a river

The currents twist
and the eddies defy
and the clear depths disguise
and the rocks conceal
and the trees stroke
the water's skin
not knowing where
to begin.

The river,
newly awake,
begs for shelter.

mafuku.

It is wartime.

In the forest
after the storm
the river is born
in the trees.

mhango.

In her hands –
the streams of life drawn
from a clear spring
high up

on the
rocky moor.

guvi.

She drinks
and the river folds itself
into her belly
months before it is born,
its story to come,
but not yet, not yet.

Time for the telling
lies downstream.
Beyond the waterfall not seen
and the waves
on a far-off neglected shore.

Here in the ruwaré
it is time for the three waters
of the source
to hide in her bone breast,
granted fragile protection
from all that may be
said
or told
too soon.

running return

vakuru vakati chinokanganwa idemo
asi muti wakatemwa haukanganwi
the proverb is a reflection that
what forgets is the axe
but the tree that was cut does not forget

the mouth of this river is dreaming of words
in dreamtime but in the meantime
it is not going swimmingly
bursting on the inside but on the outside
all we get to see is the brave face
so to ask where is the safe space
brave enough for difficult conversations
safe enough for nuanced observations
elsewhere it is just life
'racism isn't a problem in Scotland'
'oh God she's talking about racism again'
at the same time
'no matter how much I'm perceived to be loud
my voice is still not heard'
'i feel like I cannot bring my whole self
just parts that are acceptable'
and in the meantime
instead of raising instead erasing
the young talking of problem behaviour
unfair burden placed on people of colour
racial trauma leading to mental unwellness

in all this embarrassing richness
we cannot afford to ignore race
to ignore race is to ignore ourselves

we cannot afford to neglect healing
to neglect healing is to neglect learning
fundo cunoastere seekna al táleem ionnsaich
so much ground covered
so much left uncovered
in the spirit of this dear rugged land

the mouth of this cave is yawning in song
yawn time but in the dawn time
it is not going harmoniously
all we get to see is the brave face
so to ask where is the safe space
brave enough for collaboration
safe enough for cocreation
elsewhere it is just life
'i don't see colour i'm colourblind'
'i concentrate on what unites us'
but in the dawn time
'they gave me a place but don't want me
to fully occupy that space'
'i'm expected to accommodate others
so that my difference does not offend them'
and in the dawn time
instead of raising instead erasing
the young talking of problem behaviour
unfair burden placed on people of colour
racial trauma leading to mental unwellness

in all this embarrassing richness
we cannot afford to ignore race
to ignore race is to ignore ourselves
we cannot afford to neglect healing
to neglect healing is to neglect learning

fundo cunoastere seekna al táleem ionnsaich
so much ground covered
so much left uncovered
in the spirit of this dear rugged land

the mouth of a ventriloquist is dummying the run
that is dummy time but in running time
it is not going tickety-boo
all we get to see is the brave face
so to ask where is the safe space
brave enough for the insatiable search for justice
safe enough for amplifying voices trapped in brackets
elsewhere it is just life
'what does it have to do with me?'
'it's all in the past let's just move on'
and in running time
'am i good enough? i'm not good enough'
'why am i different? i don't want to be different'
and in the dawn time
instead of raising instead erasing
the young talking of problem behaviour
unfair burden placed on people of colour
racial trauma leading to mental unwellness

in all this embarrassing richness
we cannot afford to ignore race
to ignore race is to ignore ourselves
we cannot afford to neglect healing
to neglect healing is to neglect learning
fundo cunoastere seekna al táleem ionnsaich
so much ground covered
so much left uncovered
in the spirit of this dear rugged land

all we get to see is the brave face
but there is a safe brave space
a teaching and learning programme
called 'building racial literacy'
what everybody should be doing
promoting race equality and antiracist education
inclusive and supportive
where it's ok not to always stand tall
where it's ok not to always stand at all
sometimes we have to stumble a little
real is ok but i kinda like the surreal
where we take those stumbling blocks
and we turn them into building blocks

in the spirit of this dear rugged land

my habibti and i are raising two girls
and if they came one day saying
'mama baba i hate my hair, i want to be blond'
i would say 'you need to add an e after d
dictionary says that is correct female form'
……………
i wouldn't say that
i would probably tell them what they tell me
'you're sparkling on the inside'
'you have a rich culture where you come from'
'we all have varying amounts of melanin'
but they don't want to hear that
they don't want to hear that from me
they want to hear it from friends and peers
teachers neighbours and mates
they need to hear it from out there
and they may settle for now

for now is not the time to get into it
to get into what they say
'teach them to be proud of who they are'
but how can they reach for pride
when they are still figuring out
how to tie shoelaces
do and undo buttons
and they are not alone
they are just among
all who just want to belong
all children
all children of this rugged dear place
i don't want to see another brave face
i want to imbibe the vibe of ancients
the proverb is a reflection
tend to all for all have seeds inside
chenga ose manhanga hapana risina mhodzi

Commissioned for Education Scotland's 'Building Racial Literacy'
programme, 2021

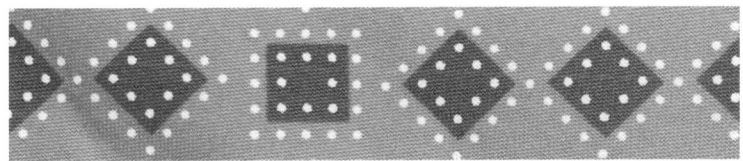

Can you hear my river?

Can you hear my river?
she asked, the sun
shafting through the old pine
trees to catch the white
rapids and then refracting
into rainbows over the spray.

Can you hear how the sun plays
through this inexorable,
gravitational tumbling rush
over stones to the sea?

Can you hear the joy
when the sun plays with the
sound waves on this, she said,
the high bank
of my own meander?

Can you hear its song?
Let me tell you it sounds like
your own heart when echoing
round the inside of the calabash
you hold to your ear.

Can you hear my river?

It is wartime in summertime.
And for once the shallows have
appeared to reveal a point of crossing

and the sound is welcome,
gentle, not a roar of danger
and flood.

She kneels on the bank,
lowers her head to drink.

There is serenity
like that of this river
in the glitter of high
sunlight. It belies
stories of suffering, told and telling,
which glisten
on her skin, and under the spell
of two rivers chanting,
and the cold taste
of nature on her lips,
are their own
intercedings for healing,
and hearing
and a hearth.

Can you hear her river?

meander

the river meanders
out of respect for the land
despite its forceful rush
its sweeping gush
the river must hush
through wonderment
acknowledge
the mountains
the desert sands
the loamy rich sands
the rock face the ruwaré
the river meanders
drawing and depositing sediment
between banks
courteously curving
and carefully carving
its own determination
own destiny
unknown destination
running and returning
between land and sea
ever running
ever returning
in the current
no two reflections are the same
the overhead sky
the overhanging branches
the various grasses
and various visitors
different drinkers

no two reflections are the same
they say baboons don't like
seeing their reflection
why they only drink at the rapids
by habit
the river meanders
rapidly now before pouring over
the cliff edge
then it is mapopoma
mafashama
mapopoma
then settling and slowing
down in the lowlands
the river meanders
no forceful rush
no sweeping gush
steady hush
shushing through the plains
the river meanders
shushing through the plains
who knows what secrets are swirling
who knows what twigs are twirling
in the winding waterway
winding
winding
twisting
winding
twisting
over time
the meandering river
turning into an oxbow lake

Crossing the Volta

The water spirits
take no prisoners.

On the islands
the snakes writhe.

You can land
and walk there
but contrary
to common speech
the island
does not belong
to the hotel.

The river spits forth plastic.
The boats sing
with the beat of the ghetto.
The continent stirs,
sluggish
and sleepy despite Her being up since dawn.
Irritated by the tin music,
She prefers the birdsong
and the palm-leaf shaker,
the stroke of the lobster paddle.

She has seen us before on this river.
White-skinned and black-skinned,
making and spending our coins,
throwing out our bridges

like ropes of progress,
heaping up gold-earthen dams
like sand-papered termite hills.

'Listen'
She whispers in a terrible tone
from deep inside the ripples.
'The birds are loyal to me,
returning from afar with every season.
They swoop away
from your grasping hands.
They circle and soar.
Sentinels.'

'Watch' She murmurs.
'Your children
all lathered in key soap
know my secrets as they

dive

through the shallows
and into
my flow.'

The river is not for coins.

weathering withering whethering

times may be the hardest
modest time is the artist
weathering the stonework
used for putting up walls
as for putting up with walls
it goes way way above

times may be the easiest
modest time is the busiest
withering the woodwork
used for putting up fences
as for putting up defences
it goes way way around

times may be the hardest
modest time is the artist
whethering stone or woodwork
used for paving pathways
as for paving walkways
it goes way way about

and there is a certain sheen
from feet polishing
the cobbled street that is
the wayfarers' thoroughfare

whether wither weather
or pelter weather
there is a certain sheen

on the cobbled street that is
the wayfarers' thoroughfare

in wither weather
there will be
yowé yowé yowé yowé
yuwi yuwi yuwi yuwi
in pelter weather
there will be
tsvédu tsvédu tsvédu tsvédu
tsvédu tsvédu tsvédu tsvédu

from feet polishing
the cobbled street that is
the wayfarers' thoroughfare

instep outstep sidestep
stride step grind step
mighty step tiny step
instep outstep sidestep

all all and more more

sheen keeping feet polishing
on the cobbled street that is
the wayfarers' thoroughfare

Written for the launch of the New Scots Refugee Integration Strategy, 2024

No matter how poisoned the land

No matter how poisoned the land
the fungus will fix everything.

Everything.

The promise of yeast
in unleavened bread
is only for days
when all is to be
destroyed.

Or when all has been lost.

Everything.

We need the taste of fungus
on our tongues.

Open your mouth and let
the yeast rise upon it.

Present the words
that bubble and breathe
with a possibility of more.

An excess.
A doubling in size.

Rot this casino,
this shopping mall world
rotten to its core.

Let the fungus moulder all.

Decay comes
from the poet's words
finding a way,
clean as a surgeon's knife
to cut to the quick
and expose all
to the air.

The air, the air,
the germs on the air
the fixers of all.
Of everything.

Energy sucks at the old host
and strengthens its hold.

Be bright toadstool,
small microbe,
be dun-coloured mushroom
or just be the fermentation
that gives us our
sourdough,
our wine.

nothing much said

knowing that one
could easily devour
consume the other
between the city
and the citizen
nothing much said

nothing much said
not to mention
pitfalls and predators
sea-saws and escalators

nothing much said
not to mention
smiles to force
things to endorse

nothing much said
not to mention
upstarting upkeeping
updating upgrading

nothing much said
not to mention
yearning to make a living
learning to make a killing

nothing much said
not to mention

trained to obey
the premier in command
and so to pay
the bearer on demand

These trees

These trees
which we planted
together,
which grew strong
with roots reaching deep
into the loamy earth.

These trees which
we tended together,
with stakes
and twine
and hours
of our time.

These trees
which blossomed
in the springtime.

These trees which
fruited in summer
and fell into our
laughing hands
staining
our mouths
sweet red.

These trees
with their

bronze and
white and
gold, with their
silver cracked bark and
smooth skin.

These trees
with their
canopy of birds and
honey hives,
their sheltering
of light and
shade.

You took an axe
sharp and straight
with no hesitation
to the heart wood.

These trees lie
across the land
mortal wounds
open
stripped bare and
rotting now.

Burn them
to cold ashes.

musasa

there is nothing special
about the musasa
after all
under any tree is shade
nothing at all special
about this musasa
just so happens to be here
on familiar ground
just so happens to be here
resting some
nesting some
within deep wrinkles
of lichen grey
scars the remains
where branches took off
rainswept
windswept
earthkept
natural rhythm
that roots remain
and leaves return
there is nothing special
about the musasa
after all
under any tree is roots
just so happens to be here
we just so happen to be here
on familiar ground

The rotting season

A mortal wound
this one.

So let the flesh cool.
Let the flesh rot.

Let rain beat
and sun bleach.

Let the putrid stench
keep you at bay.

Let the worms
work,
and the earth send
her creaturely
undertakers
to this foul feast.

Let the carrion crows
peck at the skin.

Let the robin
drink from the eyes.

Let the rats gorge
on entrails.

Let rain beat
and sun bleach.

Until the bones shine
white against a glow
of starlight
under this,
the hunter's moon.

When it is over,
and what has died is clean
and without infestation
or infection,
then we will see
what grows from
the rotting matter.

Then, and only then,
may you hold the bone,
twirling the past
between finger
and knuckle
and thumb

and stroke smooth death
and draw in your breath
and wish.

as

as air unnoticed
as lifeless until
a stir
slight cough
pushing out
as strength increasing
until
a sneeze
sweeps
petals from flowers
leaves from trees
as when in season
ripened fruits
descend from roots
as consequence
feet hooves and paws
to walk over them
beaks to prod
and scaly bellies
to crawl over them
as then skin and flesh
eaten away
and then decay
leaving inner insides
as natural
mother earth
throws herself
as cover
let them sleep
and wake
with the rain

Black in history

There are Rooks
BlackCoated still
yet harsher of song.

The Rowan,
stripped of her
BerryBlood,
curls in her leaves
and dies.

Again.
And.
Again.

The YoungPine leans
towards the woodland
roots BareCasualties
of the cruelty
of how things
just have to be.

The OldPine,
too WarBroken now
for words
or wisdom,
looks on.

On the RiverBanks
the humans still build circles
with SmoothStones,
tombs for the
BlackCharredEmbers
after the HeartFeasts
of summer.

In the Square
the Sage stands amongst
the Monuments
'Keep them'
'Write of them'
'Make them as honest
as we are able'

This was never work
for a single month
under the hunter's moon.

arc

as the sky weeps the river runs
it is the spirit of freedom
for fish to swim and bird to sing
as leaves return and roots remain

let life maintain and earth sustain

is a rusty ring hollowing hollowing hollowing
once short no longer of service
to human and non-human kin
up up caretakers of concern
sturdy stance on shifting sands

let life evolve and earth revolve

is a trusty ring engaging engaging engaging
a need to return to search again
aspire enquire perspire inspire
tending hands and attentive minds
cocreate the kind of space to find
stone for the age and glass for the sage

welcome to Mazumdar-Shaw
may the name resound and be it renowned
for energy sparking moments of discovery
for transforming lives and changing the world
the quiet of concentration and music of migration
asking what is the shumo that makes the glass glow

in addition to tradition is ambition

if this be a building very well then
impress let it impress as a fingerprint of devotion
if this be a centre very well then
gather let it gather as an old place of healing
if this be a heart very well then
beat let it beat as a multitude of eardrums
if this be an arc very well then
curve let it curve as the arms of embrace

what next spring will bring

*Commissioned by the University of Glasgow for the opening of the
Mazumdar-Shaw Advanced Research Centre*

Great northern divers

For Kat and Ruedi

Hereabouts
they call them great,
their grand name
a hymn of praise
to the lands
of the north.

Elsewhere
they are loons.
Changelings
with the seasons,
the boastful
hope of spring
now the
dove grey of
early autumn.

Black of head
white of belly
but with
no beak-clenched
olive branch
of peace.

For it is wartime.

Those who
would migrate
must huddle in
to the shoreline.

Perhaps the winter
will be kind;
perhaps she
will be cruel;
perhaps the divers
will disappear
between the waves
under the growing circles;
between battle lines
and cries
and borders;
burial cairns marking
where they once were.

Before extinction.

leathers and smartphones

imagine yourself as the protagonist
in this epic old tale
when you are born
so thrilled are the people
they call you names
if you head north you are diaspora
if you head south you are migrant
and the narrative gets more creative
in this epic old tale
of aspiration and desire
economies of prayer
prophecy and promise
of a promised land

in this epic old tale told
of the being
being on the move
being in between

looming and grooming
go go now don't go
outside influence and family
pressurising and pressure rising
higher and higher
up the hierarchy
competition and inequality
underrepresented and deeply resented
setting targets and being targeted
risks politics exploitation

distortion and extortion
protection rackets and abductions
abstract and actual violence
and the narrative gets more creative
illustrating illustrious illusions
to hide the shame of perceived failure

in this epic old tale told
of the being
being on the move
being in between

five stops on land
non-stop by air
remember the *Jordans*
and the special number 23
silver gold diamond
arrival survival revival
place making and ace trading
leathers and smartphones
and the narrative gets more creative
theory of change and cultural exchange
resistance and resilience
living it
education and entertainment
giving it
emotion and enrichment
spirited

in this epic old tale told
of the being

being on the move
being in between

origin and destination
hysteria and history
in this epic old tale
mbizi ne ngongoni
people and cattle
fishes and birds
instigation imitation irritation
tests and testimonies
welcome and unwelcome
news of newborns
bodies for burial
every life ritual
in this epic old tale
of immortalisation
down at the market
you either haggle
or you simply say
'wrap it up'

For the Ethiopia-South Africa Migration Corridor of the MIDEQ Project

Beads

For Ross

Fused and formed of sand.
Ground by the sea
from stone.
Fired,
adorned,
fitted,
fitting and strung,
they slipped from wrist
through hand and finger
to sit in stewardship
of the pulse.

The pulse took us to the sea,
swelling against the skin
moon rhythm
to blood beat.

But the beads slipped
their shackle shape
and returned as blues and yellow
as gold and green
to dive through
surf and glad GreenBlue
to the grindstone WaterWaves
of the cape of the coast.

I gave my beads to the sea.
A circle completing
[..]

a circle [...]

baddy lost goody

they had many names for him
but let's just call him goody
goody had two shoes
one for the right foot
one for the left foot
and that was how he stood
goody went walkabout
it was such a shame
someone stood on goody's foot
and a good shoe was lost
that was just too bad

goody was still very good
but now he had only one shoe
one for the right foot
nothing for the left foot
and that was how he stood
goody could no longer go walkabout
now he had to go hop-about
such a shame again
someone stood on goody's other foot
and another good shoe was lost
that was just too bad

still goody remained very good
but now he had no shoes
nothing for the right foot
nothing for the left foot

and that was how he stood
goody could no longer go walkabout
in two good shoes
goody could no longer go hop-about
in one good shoe
so he goes walkabout
on two bare feet

Part V – Freedom to praise

Wounded

When the mystics
are wounded
there is work for the healers.
A mending from
the needletouch of tenderness
through the grandfathers.

A bird limps.
Leg broken.

From the tendering of flesh
poets will find
a new tongue
for holding the WorldPain.

A breath will be born
and there will be more air for
the leaves to breathe.

Metaphors will meet in
these borderlands of brokenness
and we will recognise them
for the first time.

Today I came under
the weave of a woman
with a god's-eye gift,

under the touch
of the grandfathers,

under the mercy
of a visitation,

each a restoration
of the breath.

Tonight the moon
is plenty full.

chifumuro

Healing is revealing
here come words – breathing living churning piercing healing
damaging shaking whispering shouting
verbally invigorating

The wolf moon – and its phases

I

It is under
the full moon
of the wolf,
when the call comes
again.

There are wounds in my soul
which God probably means to leave open.

The community honours
the women it dishonours.

She stands on the crossroads
of her anger
readying herself
for the narrow way.

Narrower than ever,
now.
No track
though some have walked here
in the past,
only of that can she be sure.

Neither desert sand
nor forest track,
but rather the way
of the knife,

in the back.

II

Waxing,
the tongue
slices the skin open,
the protocols
are steady
yet seem broken,
the steel of
the red flesh-bladed tongue
drives forward through
the hardwood of time.

In the serenity of the listening,
the wound will return
and as it bleeds again
she will turn
towards the narrow way,
towards the fleshways
of life's home
to waulk the grief again.

In the stillness of the unbearing,
this is the way of unwifing,
the scars held within,
those of the denial
of a midwifing.

III

She weaves the berry-red thread
around the rowan cross,

stitching it into the skin,
and so protected,
lets her wound
be unhealed again:

And she listens to the knife cutting her.
And she listens to the words.
And she listens to the silence of
the wound opening.
And she listens to the tongue.
And she listens to spirits
of the unborn ancestral dead.

She listens to the words
behind the door that is guilt.

She listens to
her heart
beating her
with all the stories
that cannot break.

And she listens to the knife.
And she listens for the pause.
And she listens for the lifting of the knife,
and she listens for the blood,
and she listens for the secrets
as they stop,
and she listens for the heartbeat
that stopped,
and she listens for the unborn

ancestral
dead.

[…]

And her rage is
of the wolf moon.
She can hear it
howling in November.

Still
still
still
still
stilling the words
she wishes to speak,
from the wolf-howl
forming in her wide,
wild mouth.

There have been
many moon months now
of the casual use of cruelty.

Or so it has seemed.

Stillness protects
from the whip-crack
of the tongue.
Let the unborn
through

to make the peace
of women

with
the unborn
ancestral dead.

This unhealing is
for the unborn,
for the midwifing
for the anguished hope of
holding
a child,

a newborn
needing
milk.

There can be no more
speech until this
wolf moon
has waned
and the new moon
hangs

on a rowan-red
thread

in the next sky.

What led us here
will lead us through.

kuziva mbuya huudzwa
(learning comes through listening)

For librarians and caretakers of knowledge stories
everywhere

i woke up and tickled a lion
amuna wé
life is determined
in the body of knowledge
where were you when we were in awe
theatre thrives on artistic licence
and accustomed silence
those that are allowed are aloud
as they cast spells
the enchanted keep succumbing
to the s.p.e.l.l.s s.p.e.l.l.s s.p.e.l.l.s
the enchanted keep succumbing
to the feeling of kneeling
at the altercation of stories
panotsva demo mupinyi uchisara
wordplay like swordplay
firebreathers and swashbucklers
frostbiters and mass smugglers
close call and far-fetched
at the altercation of stories
author's pen and artist's pencil
priszed by avid antagonists
strapped on as makeshift stilts
to teeter teeter teeter and tower
in desperation for elevation
at the altercation of stories

author's pen and artist's pencil
priszed by avid antagonists
scratched on as ambitious drawwings
to flap flap flap and fly
in desperation for elevation
panotsva demo mupinyi uchisara

i spent the day nudging wasps
amuna wé
life is determined
in the body of knowledge
where were you when we were in awe
theatre thrives on pure dramatics
and sound acoustics
those that are sound are the raconteur
as they entrance
the enchanted fulfil the entrance
to the moving vividworld
of their own picturing
volume velocity variety
volume velocity variety
line up and move *in*formation
hakudanwi anonzwa
it's a wobbly entrance i mean entrance
but before you know it
hapless hopeful meets helpful guide
but the wisdom entered
has not been recognised
but before you know it
it's the book of ancient spells
but comes unstuck on g.l.u.e.
trundles on insufficient data bundles
but before you know it

love sings and war cries
elation
elevation to the sky
to return to the main menu
press star
hakudanwi anonzwa

i rose up and hugged an eagle
amuna wé
life is determined
in the body of knowledge
where were you when we were in awe
theatre thrives onstage
and backstage
those that make it make it possible
as they do the rigging
the enchanted cannot help it
spontaneity of the jigging
shelving inhibition
delving into exhibition
chains change and unsettled objects
simbai tizwe vabati vebasa
what would the whoosh of the magic express
be without a conductor
maintaining poise in the swervy sway
of pondering pasts and figuring futures
crossing with you with nothing to declare
so it's only fair to pay your fare
what would the whoosh of a classic concert
be without a conductor
to disambiguate the timbres
from sensational tones of those who purvey
to unemotional tones of the ordinance survey

what would the whoosh of electricity be
without a conductor
response ability elasticity
whatever the current eccentricity
life is determined in the body of knowledge
where were you when we were in awe
of the reassuring frown of
detective without crime
strict without sting
grace without fatigue
apothecary minds sanctuary
lending attending tending
to be kind just kind
lending attending tending
to be lifelines
simbai tizwe vabati vebasa

i got down and pinched a shark
amuna wé
life is determined
in the body of knowledge
where were you when we were in awe
theatre thrives on weighted blankets
and suspended beliefs
those who are weighted are waited on
as they try to order
seeings beings believings
the enchanted view open lexicon
but if the definition is *de*meaning
the early bird catches the bookworm
kuziva mbuya huudzwa
between the home and the field

a road is built a path is ground
dust rises to the rhythm of eardrums
free spirit is not a description
but earnest protest
free spirit
overdue return remains outstanding
as cave wall is to touchscreen
the earliest library was a librarian
the oldest archive still survives
pasichigaré our living nature
everything known is borrowed
everything owned is given
life is determined
in the body of knowledge
where were we when we were in awe
kuziva mbuya huudzwa

Glossary

amuna wé – my dear family
panotsva demo mupinyi uchisara – proverb saying unbelievable
things will happen
hakudanwi anonzwa – proverb saying exciting things happen
for all to see
simbai tizwe vabati vebasa – stay steady, bearers of the work
pasichigaré – the ancient approach to life where all nature is a
family

*Commissioned for the incorporation of the African Chapter of the
Association of Information Sciences and Technology, 2023*

Look!

Look! Look!
There on the horizon
the long white cloud
for which
I am longing.

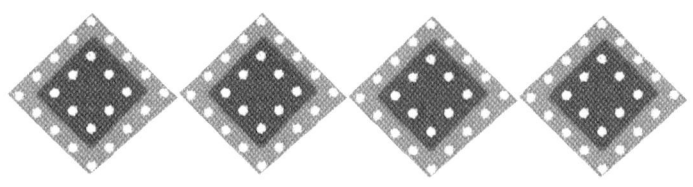

every now and again

every now and again
the sky dusts the earth
with a little reign

A day as full as the moon

A day as full as the moon.
No silver crack through which
the gods offer gifts,
simply a bathing in light.

The battle behind us,
the war still tugging
but on another shore,

as are heart pieces
and the people held in a web
of border corruption
and tangled deceit.

They are as present to us
as the breathing child on my lap
as close and tightly held as
the greetings which race
breathlessly towards us
screaming for joy.

Sometimes a gift is given
and not received.

Sometimes it is received so deeply
that as the full moon
is our witness
there is
no greater abundance
than what it becomes.

jenaguru

the magnificent moonlight
they say it was spoken of this
in the grand days of time
illuminated beneath open skies
the truth is stark
nature exposing
secrets of the dark
knowledge dissolved in daylight
wisdom dissolved in moonlight
the magnificent moonlight
jenaguru

Poor in spirit

By the end she was
poor in spirit.
Spent.

The bloodletting had been controlled at first,
the sacrifice steady,
few murmurs of distress,
but as time passed the realisation
of the spirit-price to be paid became
clear as the water
from the January spring.

A vein opened,
then another,
rich seams of red
for our clothing.

The music of the mournings
held us all, for as long as the beat
was deep.
But in the silence of our evenings
we fell to the earth.

And the makers asked again
for the breaking of the
shell that held
the spirit.

And the spirit was released into the river.
And the spirit was hidden in the hills.

And the spirit met the skies and trees and the leaves.

And the snakes came.
And the scorpions came.
And the powers of destruction
did their worst.

Fire came.
Flood came.
Blood, always the blood.

And the spirit flooded from her soul.
And the spirit flooded from her heart.
And the spirit of her intellect emptied
all that it had.

And love left and the spirits walked
from her feet.

And the spirit of her body
grew in knowledge
and in strength.

By the end,
poor in spirit.
Spent.

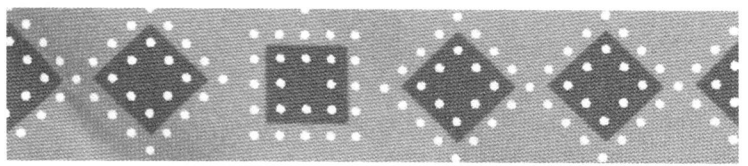

rupture

an uneventful happening
slapped faces of clocks
waved hands of time
no twinkling skies
no smiling
the poles flagging at half mast
pangaea was from another era
parts walked away to make more
collided with futures unpredicted
impact
reverberating through hungry earth
the equator lies arched
oceans lie parched
great rivers go thirsty
before they reach the beach
come to a sudden screech
fantastic voices quick-sinking
volumes to be told
embodiment of nature
now the main attraction
in a cage of a zoo
birds with heavy wings
cursed with every swing
the calibrated pendulum
agony far on the horizon
sunrays like heat waves
daybreaks like heartaches
headaches like earthquakes
rainbows like chainsaws
grains of maize shudder in cobs

eerie sounds of spinning cogs
whatever next to expect
but still push out a brave limb
soon better in retrospect
introspection's reflection
casts a shadow over doubtless minds
cloudless lives
a shadow, over an already dark day
April was relieved, with sadness
to see the arrival of May
over in the cold
they were begging for ice
over in the desert
they were begging for sand
over in the forest
they were begging for twigs
something was missing

The HeartBeats

The heart
Beats

Makes
Breaks
Beats
Makes
Breaks
Beats

And makes
And breaks
And makes
And breaks.

Ruled by fear
You made fear into
Rules.

Breaks
Makes.

For fear of
The rules
The heart

Makes

Breaks.

Fear rules.
The heart
Beats.

The wideness
Narrow now
Dark with shadows,
The wildness
Cowering under
The strain of
Restraint.

Time breaks
Beats
Makes

Beats.

This is not how
It feels
But how it felt.

urban tears

crying urban tears
in a stony environment
not wanting to be found
finders stay away
not wanting to be held
capturers stay away
reality is here
but not fully present
smiles all round
but not fully pleasant
on the stage of life
playing a role
discreet thinkers
playing the fool
so that healing can occur
from within
possessions of life
held tight in a clenched fist
but careless hearts
jarring with each turn
trains of thought
travelling at a great velocity
terminal to terminal
but no arrival
coz ideas never really took off
the real theatre of dreams
needs a showcase
from time to time

no harm in dreamy feet
slipping into reality
from time to time
we sit in contemplation
and meditation
anguish in this time
we take a lot
sometimes a little
sometimes take it in moderation
sometimes don't take it at all
pondering thoughts
sometimes stray
onto the memories
of those who have passed away
and then these doubts
get cast away
aches and pains
tossed away
while we cry these dry tears
finders better stay away
we don't want to be found
and capturers better stay away
we don't want to be held
not now
not any more

The earth is covered in darkness

Even as wartime fades,
music spread her
deep power across the universe
and filled a calabash
with fire from the gods.

There was joy
and ecstasy in the young
and a dance
which kissed the heavens
with the gift of
the defiant repenting people
of the broken words on earth.

But the mystic makers of the dream
knew the price they had paid
in silver, sacrifice and soul
and in them, at first,
in the aftermath of the victory,
only the dull hollow
ache of defeat.

In them

loss is plentiful.

The earth is covered in darkness.

Loss of hold, and hunger.
Loss of life and loveliness.

Loss of the common cup
and the calabash.

You cannot wrestle
such a blessing
unscathed.

Unless a grain of wheat
falls to the earth and dies,
it remains

alone.

The promise in death
of plenty.

Sickness and sadness
must first exact
their heavy reparations,
and hearts must be searched
for meaning,
and prayers must be said
to heal
and clear a space
for forgiveness,
for the harsh words
of love,
which came
when horror was
rotting the kernel of all hope,

and breath left the spirit's husk
and has yet to return.

The earth is covered in darkness.

There is a garden.

Birdsong.

Trees and silence.
A warmth is in the autumnal sun
under the blue northern sky
of harvest time
and a fox
is my amber-coated witness.

It is here that
the earth will give
of the smooth-skinned echo chambers
and music will join words
as song
to tell of this war
too,

in ways which are silent
and ways which are true.

The earth is covered in darkness.

the spirit of darkness

the spirit of darkness
will lead you to DoomSo
what will you do
when it comes
testing the faith
of who you worship
testing the faith
of you who worship
that old water deity
mighty hydroelectricity
whether you close eyes
or open mind
best believe
everyone is a believer

the spirit of darkness
will lead you to DoomSo
what will you do
when it strikes
right at the heart of
every single appliance
of your power alliance
your powerful defences
are breaking
and entering
is the opposite of lightning
snatching your lighting
stealing your convenience
possessing your home

the spirit of darkness
will lead you to DoomSo
what will you do
when it takes
hold and blood runs cold
as the river of electrons
suddenly stops flowing
in this untoward standstill
you will be moved
you will feel the power
as you feel your way
in inky dinky room
turned off you're turned into
venerator of the generator

the spirit of darkness
will lead you to DoomSo
what will you do
when it descends
then sends you back
to the flames
and at the fireside
to rediscover
an ancestor on the inside
to a time before a time before
in absence of the current
all turns rustic and acoustic
sun and moon order the day
all the way back to nature

the spirit of darkness
will lead you to GloomSo

what will you do
what will you do with gloom
what will you do with doom
what will you do with DoomSo
what will you do

'Dumsor' is one word used for the power outages, 'load shedding' and power 'cuts' that many of our colleagues experience in their day-to-day work.

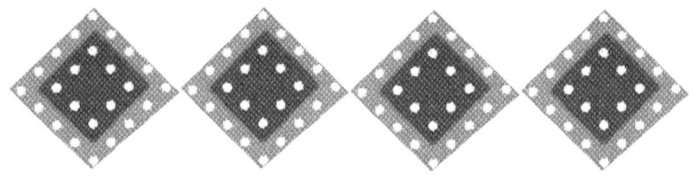

Night watching

By day the river had been
broad, brown, deep.
And the road, shall we say,
surprising,
with its looms
and elephant grass
and palm wine.

By night
the stars were begging
to be courted.

The trees, guardians
of nature's deep
wisdom. The earth,
warm. The breath,
a bountiful breeze.

There was also the moon
glancing down
with a kindliness, born
of NightWatching.

An unsettled,
mysterious peace,
spinning the silver time
of old moonlight and dying starlight
into a gossamer thread, with
which we might weave cloth
enough to clothe
the outer skin of dreamtime
and live within
the longing for a little more
of the bright
beauty of conversation
woven from the words
that nurture
the mystic's soul.

do hesitate to

do hesitate to
touch the head
do hesitate to
touch the feet
uncanny bodily knowledges
do hesitate to
enter the sango/forest
do hesitate to
touch the zvimerwa/plants
do hesitate to
utter mazwi/words
uncanny bodily knowledges
tandavara
open up to kunaya/healing
munzwa unotumburwa neumwe munzwa
is an ancient saying
a thorn is removed by another thorn
tandavara
open up to the myst
open wide to
a twist of gist

Blessing

A rowan tree
for each corner
of your four directions.

And here is sage
pungent,
medicinal,
pure
to smudge
and cense
your soul.

I give you willow
for humility.
Bending you low
into the earth.
Graceful as each greeting
for friend,
for family,
for foe.

Then to gentle
a traveller's weariness:
lavender.
And birch oil
for the smoothing
of skin, and longing,
and bone.

crannog means shama

faìlte hekani marhaba welcome
the invitation of mystics
faìlte hekani marhaba welcome
passwords to pathways laid before us
ancestors are not done
we are what they have become
keeping the fire lit in the firepit
come in come on come now
the invocation of mischief
shall we see what happens
when we assume fearless poise
far from the nearest noise
chance of getting spirited away
drink depths to quench questions
immersed in everyday wonder
of the forest growing alder
winged singers of mountains
the tide washes the shoreline
simple things keep things simple
on two thumbs we do sums
life plus style folk times lore
the tide traces the shoreline
clay is dimpled play is kindled
if you thought you were at home
well you're not mistaken
here fingerprints are left or felt
not taken
what weavers fashion is felt
textiles couldn't be in better hands

what weavers fashion is felt
exiles couldn't be in better hands
crannog means shama means shelter means more
indigenous ways these ingenious ways
technology of carving shadows
archaeology of unearthing stories
in this round house raised on water
then the pain of being razed by fire
then rebuilt refurbished refurnished
all by a thousand touches
all in a thousand voices
all in the presence of nature
the ancient power of water
to gather all creatures
water living and water loving
on the shoreline
and there was a spirit woman
deep down dwellers know
she was keening
she was keening
and in maungira
we were recalling
remembering our shimmering

Commissioned for the opening of the new Crannog Centre at Dalerb, 31st March, 2024

At Nehanda's tree

At Nehanda's tree
the boys sell onions,
top-ups
and cheap plastic imports
from China.

They are advertising
stump dressing

and the killing of bees.

the station area

we are sorry to announce that
the
1948
service to
equality in rights and dignity
is delayed by approximately
countless minutes
of countless meetings
please listen
for further announcements

the next train at platform
3
will be the delayed
1945
service to
unity
peace and security

if you see
anything suspicious
please report
to a member of staff

passengers are kindly reminded
it is not permitted
to dance
smoke
or make love
in the station area

the train now arriving at
platform
4
is the
shuttle service
to
71 nations and territories
representing a third of
the world's total population
this service is running on time

delays are expected
on the
southern line
due to ongoing
signalling problems

the train now at platform
2
is the delayed
2000
service to
a better and
more sustainable
future
this train is now expected
to depart at
2015

due to adverse weather conditions
surfaces may be slippery
passengers are kindly reminded
to take extra care
in the station area

we are sorry to announce that
the
1948
service to
equality in dignity and rights
is delayed by approximately
countless minutes
of countless meetings
please listen
for further announcements

passengers are kindly reminded
it is not permitted
to dance
smoke
or make love
in the station area

Epilogue – Warriors cry

We are nature: pasichigaré

I am announcing the Advent
of an OldNew Way.

Corridors which are recognisable
as the world's roadways
have underground passages,
interlacings and entwinements
of the spirits.

Our task,
what we are for,
who I am,
who we are,
is clear
as the spring water
from beneath the granite rock,
from within the softenings of the porous stone.

The dream has returned.

Dreamtime is Daytime.

Our time.

This time.

AroAro.

The dream from the time
with the unborn ancestral dead.

Our work is in gratitude,
and GriefLove,
in giving, and grafting,
and growth.

Our work is
to listen …
Listen …
Listen …
for the echoes.

Echoes …

Echoes …

to follow the entwinements,
the rootways,
and the breeze
that tells
of the ways taken
by the birds,
and the reaching
of the leaves,
and to keep them alive
and unconceal them when the time is right,
to bring the powers
we custode to bear
on the sufferings of the earth
and her people,
the water and her ways,
the skies,

the great clouds,
the long white cloud and the starline.

Our highways and byways
will be the difference
between the clear path
and the carpet road home.

Our byways begin here in the meetings of these spirits;
the love of these old ways,
the footsteps,
the footprints,
the bare feet against the bare stones.

The vessels:
The Calabash
The Dende
The Chimi
The Quaich,
for creation,
The Hari for the well.

For the being Wel.

The way of the loom-makers
and the shearers.
The spinners
and the wool-weaving women.

We are warp and weft.

We are to be channels for the ancients
through the fire in our bones.

And my bones will rise again.

The hunger in our bellies.
The drumbeat in the bone cage
of our hearts
which we hear …

echoes …

a deep call and response.

Words.
No words.
Words.
No words.
Worlds.
No worlds.
Skies.

The birds are our guides
for the ways of the sky.
They know no borders.

The creatures of the underearth
will show us where the roots defy
all the wickedness of separation
and the darkness that it necessitates.

The trees,
the birch
and the rowan,
and the oak,

and the hawthorn,
will grow and guard our way.

The muchakata tree will drop her healing
and stroke the skin
where the pain is had and held.

The musasa tree will gather in
all the birds passing by,
all the weary ones seeking shade.
And in her shelter they will rest,
and they will mend.

The hunters will wake before dawn
searching out the food for the travellers.
The gatherers will wander the shoreline,
the forests' edge
and there shall be fish and fruits.

In the land laid waste at the homestead
there will be drumming
and music.
There will be singing
and the sounds of birdsong as the trees return
and with them the abundance of harvest.

This is love's labour.
This is love's scattering.
This is the mystic seed for each story.
This is the SourHerb and the SweetFruit.

In the rock are the stone peckings of play.

In the place no one is taken
is red earth.
And the meeting of many tides,
of grieving and rejoicing,
of longing and loving,
of hoping and healing,

and the ways for the eyes to roam in worship
in darkness of humility
and defiance that is praise.

In this place.
In this time.
In this
warriors cry.

Written after a visit to the UNESCO World Heritage Site, Great Zimbabwe

pasichigaré: we are nature

how was your day
day before yesterday
we would celebrate to relate
we were nature
now the conflict is to see the scribe describe the tribe
but i don't have a tribe
i don't have pride
those who know me better call me
ganyamatopé dzapasi
in the language of birds
words just sound
should i speak
some things done from memory
some things done by heart
the tortoise is airborne
eyes don't know what they see
i am just not myself
possessed with natural powers
how on earth do they play
this music that
makes ancients stampede
as hunters do
hunters don't
hunt the same
on this hunter's bow
the young string needs to be taut
despite who in spite do
on these footprints we withstand
so who scares

only shake when shaking to the beat
as warriors do
warriors don't
fight the same
in this warrior's cry
fears drop in place of teardrops
the aural tradition
burning bright with life
sun setting the scene
simmering esteem
what is prepared here
is not for the tender-hearted

so we count stones
as time adds bones
though we stand on
rely on
our eldest ancestor
we forget nature
we start believing
we discard instinct
lies get older
start resembling the truth
through neglect and lack of respect
the unattended field of humility
now overgrown into a forest of pride
now every action is a chain reaction
celebrating the progress of mankind
while
woman and kindness are left behind
let everyone flourish
would not be

the wish of the selfish
feeling like
we are just ourselves
brimming with confidence
so we strike conversations
and we burn like matches
our relations the trapped trees
trespassing on stolen property
so they wither like hope
in the uncovered sun
in absence of the ancients' stampede
this new manoeuvre is not like
muchongoyo
if we tended the
muchakata
perhaps we would be
shocked
disappointed
hit by realisation that
those we thought had fallen
had only fallen in our esteem
so it may seem
it is the nature of time
short as a life
long as a memory

don't remember my first name
my last name
there is a name
that comes before my first name

after my last name
ganyamatopé dzapasi
then after that more names
dambachirashwa
moyo chirandu
then after that no names
don't remember my age
remember the ages
don't remember how i look
remember how we look
alike
don't remember my words
remember the disturbing bark
of the familiar tree
rooted to earth reasons
why seeds don't decay
though the shell is eaten away
don't remember me
remember we
are nature
pasichigaré
so
don't remember me
remember to remember
what seemed long forgotten
don't remember this moment
in time
in time
swim from these shallow waters
to deep sleep
don't follow me

don't look for me
find me
in a place in time
oh well
in a place in time

Written for the permanent World Cultures Exhibit in Kelvingrove Museum and Art Gallery, 2018

Acknowledgements

We wish to acknowledge the many colleagues, friends, family members, mystics and fellow travellers who have been companions, wayfarers and witnesses throughout the making of this work. Without the generous hospitality and provisioning, with food, with shelter, with wisdom and with adventures, the borders crossed in the making of this anthology would not have been made again in poetry.

Without the administrative care of Lauren Roberts, Jennifer McArthur, Bella Hoogeveen and Brittnee Leysen the journeys could not have been taken.

The hostings and poetic promptings of the following friends and colleagues, in no special order, brought words and shapes and forms for which we are full of gratitude:

Hyab Yohannes, Maria Grazia Imperiale, Giovanna Fassetta, Heaven Crawley, Charles Forsdick, Kofi Anyidoho, Nazmi Al Masri; Ignite Theatre Company; Nii Tete Yartey and Noyam Institute for African Dance; Centre for Migration Studies; Legon, Ghana; Lit-FEST Harare; Chipawo Theatre Company, Harare; Collectivas, Mexico; MIDEQ; AMIF and CUSP Project colleagues, our colleagues in the UNESCO Chair at the University of Glasgow; The Seedling, Dunedin; Seeds of Thought; the Iona Community. We also thank our readers and elders, Aine McAllister and Mike Gonzalez, Deirdre Ford and Avril Bellinger.

The opportunity to perform, air and interrupt with the poetry that appears in this collection was generously provided by University of Glasgow; Modern Languages Association of America (MLA); British Association of Applied Linguistics; Durham University; Leeds University; Cambridge University; Oxford University; International Association for the Study of Forced Migration; Hong Kong Polytechnic University PAIR Distinguished Lecture; ArtLab UNESCO; University of New South Wales, Australia; University of South Australia; Centre for Contemporary Arts Glasgow; Islamic University of Gaza; University College London; Cologne University; Pennsylvania State University; University of East Anglia; Anglia Ruskin University; Universities of Sanctuary; University of Addis Ababa; Te Whaiti School, Te Urewhera; Auckland University of Technology; Auckland University; Victoria University Wellington; University of Waterloo, Canada; The Scottish Crannog Centre; Royal Society of Edinburgh; World Refugee Day Lecture; University of Edinburgh; Charles O'Neil Lecture; African Union; Scottish Catholic Laity Network; the Iona Community Lecture; Lancaster University; Universidade Nova, Lisbon; Literacy Education and Second Language Learning for Adults (LESLLA); Association of Commonwealth Universities; The Crichton Lectures; University of Glasgow (Dumfries); Kloster Eberbach, Universität Köln; Association for Information Science and Technology; Education Scotland; University College London; University of Ulster; Glasgow School of Art; Royal Conservatoire Scotland; Association for Applied Linguistics and Professional Practice; Association of University Language Communities, Joy Northcott Memorial Lecture, University of Edinburgh.

In particular, Alison wishes to acknowledge the generous invitation from the University of Otago – Ōtākou Whakaihu Waka – to be their De Carle Fellow, 2019, and 8 months spent honing an early draft and learning from manuwhenua and manuhiri – māori and refugee communities. Angela McCarthy, Vivienne Anderson, Kevin Fleury, Jono and Julie Ryan, Peter Matheson and Heinke Somer Matheson, Piki Diamond and Chaz Doherty were particular supports through their practical and poetic presence.

To all at Wild Goose Publications: our humble thanks for working with these words and publishing them on your beautiful pages.

For those who remained at home with their love as we travelled, wrote, made and spirited forth the work – Tarneem, Neeya and Aya; Robert, Rima, Sienna, Sion, Sean – words for sufficient gratitude continue to fail us – as they should.

We acknowledge the funding, cutting and re-funding of the research underpinning the publication of this anthology by the UK Arts and Humanities Research Council Global Challenge Research Fund; also funding from the University of Glasgow for the UNESCO Chair for Refugee Integration through Education, Languages and Arts. This specifically includes the following two awards: UK Arts and Humanities Research Council under the Culture for Inclusive and Sustainable Peace (CUSP N+) Grant Scheme (AH/T007931/1). Economic and Social Research Council South-South Migration Inequality and Development Hub (MIDEQ) Grant Scheme (Grant reference ES/S007415/1) and previously under Arts & Humanities Research Council Translating Cultures Large Grant: Researching Multilingually at the Borders of Language, the Body, Law and the State. AHRC (Grant Ref: AH/L006936/1).

About the authors

Tawona Sitholé, better known as Ganyamatopé Dzapasi, is an acclaimed poet and storyteller who has performed work worldwide. He is presently working as lecturer and artist in residence with the UNESCO Chair at the University of Glasgow, where this anthology was produced.

Alison Phipps is UNESCO Chair for Refugee Integration through Education, Languages and the Arts. She is a member of the Iona Community and a well-known broadcaster, writer, academic, activist and performer. Much of the poetry in this anthology has grown out of the projects she leads.